Wilderness to Lake Success:

History of a Village

by
Jack Binder
Village Historian

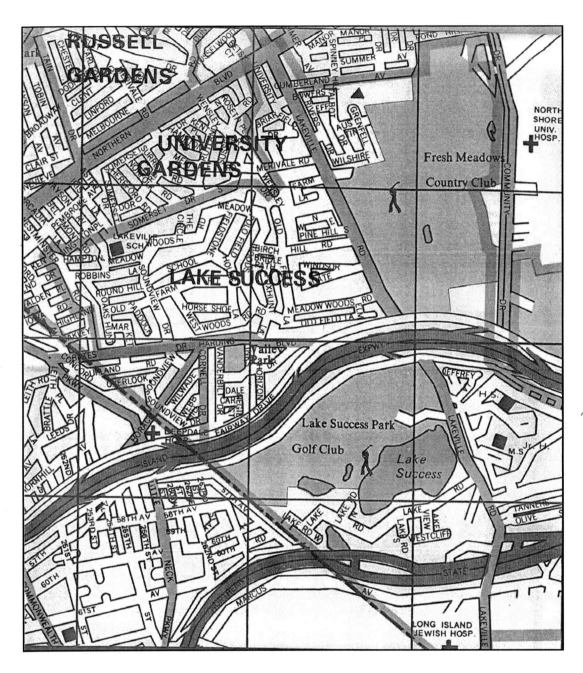

This book has been published with the support of
the Incorporated Village of Lake Success and the Lake Success Civic Association.

ISBN 0-9755968-0-2

Contents

Lakeville Road, Great Neck, L. I., Bermudez Penetration 1912

(Queens Borough Public Library)

Preface

"Life must be lived forwards but can only be understood backwards." (S. A. Kierkegaard)

Already in print are two histories of the Village of Lake Success, published in 1949 and 1968, both of which are primary source materials in public libraries. I am indebted to Robert Danzer and Kate Van Bloem, who paved the way.

Several years ago, my interest in local history was kindled when I enrolled in a class, Historic Preservation, at Adelphi University. On my bookshelf, at home in Lake Success, was a copy of Kate Van Bloem's history, which had been presented to me by the Village, in 1970, to welcome me as a new resident. I read it once again and wanted to know more. I began my research at the Great Neck Library and at the Nassau County Long Island Studies Institute. Before I knew it, I was appointed Village Historian. I broadened my search. I uncovered material which was not included in the earlier histories and decided to write a third history of the Village of Lake Success.

My wife, Margery, became my partner in this project. While I researched and wrote, she became my editor, helping with revisions. Her computer skills enabled her to use a desktop publishing program for the layout and graphic design of the book. Together, we made this book a reality.

Jack Binder

Lake Success, New York
July 2004

Prehistory

The rolling, hilly terrain of Lake Success was shaped by the advance and retreat of four glaciers over many thousands of years. The last of these glaciers, the Wisconsin, was given its name because its deposits exist today as far west as that state. Glaciation began when Earth was in a cool cycle so the snows of the winter did not melt completely in the summer. Eventually, the snow accumulation came to several thousand feet. The pressure of the heavy layer of snow turned the snow on the bottom into ice. In time, this ice became a thick liquid, allowing the mass of snow to move. A glacier was born.

Drawing by Robert Danzer

The Wisconsin glacier moved from north to south, incorporating rocks into its mass. As the glacier moved across bedrock, the rocks acted as sandpaper, producing a fine dust of clay. The farthest south the glacier advanced in the Lake Success area was where the Northern State Parkway is today. This explains why the Great Neck peninsula is hilly, while the area to the south is flat. When the climate warmed, the glacier melted, leaving behind its moraine (rock and clay). This became the soil of Lake Success.

As the glacier melted, it developed large fissures. A huge chunk of ice broke off, plunged to the bare ground and created a large depression. Because the heavy clay soil did not permit drainage, melting waters filled the depression. A lake was formed, fed by surrounding streams. This "kettle" lake is our Lake Success.

Early Settlement

The settlement of Long Island by native Americans began about five thousand years ago. The Matinecocks, a tribe of Algonquin Indians, inhabited the area around Lake Success. They roamed the forests from Flushing to Oyster Bay.

Early in the seventeenth century, the Dutch came to the Lake Success area, which they called "the wilderness." One early reference to the name Success in town records is in a deed dated September 22, 1679, for land owned by Richard Cornell. Another, dated February 1, 1683, states that John Seman was hired by the Town to survey three acres of land lying on "ye south side ye greate pond commonly called sucses." This was a corruption

of "Sacut," an Indian name which means "at an outlet of a pond." The community called itself Success until 1835, when the residents changed the name to Lakeville.

Following the Dutch, people of English descent settled in the Lake Success area. The history of the Woolley family illustrates this migration. Robert Woolley emigrated from England in 1639 and settled in Fairfield, Connecticut. In 1654, he moved to Setauket. This was a short distance across Long Island Sound from Connecticut and was the route many English people took to settle the eastern part of Long Island. Captain John Woolley bought land in the Great Neck area in the mid-eighteenth century. During the Revolutionary War, there was friction between the Dutch, who were for independence, and the loyalist English. Thomas Woolley was jailed for refusing to bear arms for the revolutionary cause.

The Woolley family history continues with brothers John and Stocker buying 141 acres near Success Lake in 1814. They built a large farmhouse which was the family dwelling until 1955, when it was sold. It is still in use as a residence today. The barn on its property was torn down in 1967. The house can be seen on Old Lakeville Road.

Icehouse, 2003

Woolley house, 2003

In the eighteenth and nineteenth centuries, Lake Success was a thriving community. Around the lake were several farms, with orchards and sheep. In addition, there was a blacksmith shop, a cider mill, a country store, a schoolhouse, a Dutch Reformed Church, and a Friends Meeting House.

In the winter, children skated on the lake. Ice was cut out and stored in sawdust in icehouses for summer use. One of these icehouses survives at the Woolley house. In the summer, there was good fishing and swimming in the lake. The lake's clear water was used when the wells ran dry. Cattle and horses were watered there, as well.

Woolley barn, circa 1900
Roof of icehouse visible at left
(Courtesy, Cecil and Estelle Jaffe)

Woolley barn, 1965
Same tree as in the 1900 photo
Tree still stands today

Woolley house, circa 1900
(Courtesy, Cecil and Estelle Jaffe)

In 1732, the first public building, the Dutch Reformed Church, was erected east of the lake. It was the largest church in Queens County, fifty feet by sixty feet. During the Revolutionary War, it was a headquarters for the British army. A Hessian camp was also nearby. In 1784, the Church served briefly as the Queens County Courthouse. Across from the Church, at the southeast corner of the lake, was a tavern owned by I. U. Willets.

Parishioners left their horses there before services and patronized the tavern afterward.

In the 1820s, attendance at the church diminished. In 1829, the building was torn down. On the original 1732 foundation, a new building was constructed. It stands today as the Marion Wiles house on the campus of the Great Neck South secondary schools. Named in memory of a respected long-time administrator of the school district, it is used now for Pupil Personnel Services.

Marion Wiles house, 1959

Wiles house, 2004

Later Settlement

"Lakeville has long been a place much resorted to and greatly admired by the lovers of natural scenery ... and it cannot fail to become a still more interesting spot to those who appreciate the pleasures of country life and delight to revel in all its luxuriance of landscape so beautifully displayed." (Benjamin Thompson describing Lake Success, 1839, "History of Long Island")

Lake Success, 1902
(Suffolk County Historical Society)

Guests from as far away as Manhattan traveled on the Jamaica-Roslyn Road to stay at local hotels. Lakeville House, built in 1843, was located at the present site of the Lake Success community building. It survived until the first decade of the twentieth century when William Vanderbilt II bought the property and tore it down.

Lakeville House, circa 1900
(Suffolk County Historical Society)

A general store was located on the present-day North Service Road of the Long Island Expressway, east of Lakeville Road. This building was expanded to become the Elverton Inn, later renamed the Red Lion Inn. It was famous for its cuisine and was supposedly a favorite of the Prince of Wales, who became King Edward VIII. In 1925, the Inn advertised furnished apartments and rooms with food service for $25 per week. The Inn provided music for dancing. A fire in 1935 destroyed the property.

Lake Success Hotel, undated
(Queens Borough Public Library)

Red Lion Inn, 1925
(New York Public Library)

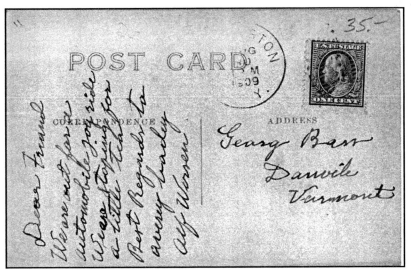

Elverton Inn, 1909
Postcard, front and back
(Collection of Al Velocci)

East of the Red Lion Inn, the Cox-Chapman farmhouse was converted into the Lakeville Manor Inn, early in the twentieth century. The building deteriorated and was torn down in the 1990s.

Lakeville Manor Inn, 1930s (Collection of Al Velocci)

In the late nineteenth century, Aunt Hannah Chisholm served her famous chicken dinners in her house at the southwest side of the lake. She was put out of business in 1902 when William Vanderbilt II bought most of the property around the lake.

Aunt Hannah's well, 1901
Her daughter on right,
with wife and daughter of photographer
(Fullerton Collection,
Suffolk County Historical Society)

The oldest remaining house in Lake Success is on Round Hill Road. What is seen from the street today was originally the rear of the house. It consisted of only one room when it was built around 1750. Another room and a porch were added in 1790. Its two-story wing was built in 1825. The original land, owned by Thomas Hicks, remained in the Hicks family until Samuel Willetts bought it in 1859.

House on Round Hill Road, May 1924
Enlarged detail below
(New York Public Library)

2003

Later, the Rice family turned the property into a horse farm where summer horse shows, called "Oaks Hunts," were held in the 1930s and 1940s. Shortly thereafter, Newell and Daniel, the builders, used the Rice farmhouse as a sales office while they constructed many homes in Lake Success. In 1953, they sold the house.

THE PERFECT SETTING
FOR A PERFECT HOME

This glorious woodland, opened last week, is now a pageant of colors. Already several locations have been selected. We invite you to see the superbly detailed Early American homes now being completed... faithfully reproducing the grace and charm of inherited designs... dramatic reminders of the past, dynamic forerunners of the future. See these beautiful Colonial Country Estates in this new woodland setting. Prices from $10,500, down payment $1000.

Orders taken now for spring delivery. Four homes are ready for your inspection and immediate occupancy.

Newell & Daniel

Lakeville Road bet. World's Fair Blvd Ext. & Northern Blvd. LAKE SUCCESS adj. Great Neck, L. I.

New York Times
September 29, 1940

The only industrial enterprise in Lake Success in the nineteenth century was Lombardo's lumber mill. Garden City's Cathedral was built in 1877 with lumber from the mill. Adjacent to the mill, Lombardo built an ornate Victorian home for his wife and fourteen children. It stood along Lakeville Road, about two hundred feet south of what is now University Road. The home was demolished in 1945. In 1947, thirty-three houses were built on the Lombardo site; this section is called Briarfield. A stone retaining wall from the Lombardo property remains in the backyard of one of these homes.

James L'Hommedieu was a notable resident of Lake Success in the late nineteenth century. His home was in the vicinity of present-day Wilshire. Munsell's History of Queens County (1882) describes it as elegant, "on the Middle Neck road, leading from the Great Neck steamboat landing to Hyde Park." The account notes his "architectural talent." L'Hommedieu is especially known for erecting every building, except five, in Garden City, in his time, and for the construction of the Cathedral. He worked closely with A.T. Stewart (Stewart Avenue) and Henry Hilton (Hilton Avenue).

1833-1892

The Williams house, at 350 Lakeville Road, still stands. It was built around 1873, on land bought from the Woolley family, the neighbor to the north. Later, William Vanderbilt II bought it to use as a guesthouse. Today, it is owned by the Lake Success Jewish Center.

Williams house, 2004

The Judge David Provost house, built around 1800, was located in what is now Windsor Gate. Its last resident was Emily Jones. In her later years, the house fell into disrepair. When Mrs. Jones died, sometime around 1990, the house and its barn were demolished. A very large house was built in their place. The new house was used as a set for the movie, "The Preacher's Wife," with Whitney Houston and Denzel Washington.

Across Lakeville Road from the Provost house was the home of the farm's overseer. In the 1950s, it was purchased by the North Shore Presbyterian Church. In 1965, the building was torn down and the present church was erected.

Jones house, circa 1965

Overseer's house as a church, circa 1964

1873

Thorne House (later, first Village Hall),
S. Willets home (now on Round Hill Road)
D. Provost home (now Windsor Gate and Presbyterian Church)
Maple Cottage and L'Hommedieu residence
Woolley property
W. Van Nostrand property, southeast of the lake (now i.park)

Maple Cottage

About 1814, Sam Warren purchased property in the vicinity of the present-day Farm Lane and on it he built a one-story farmhouse. The Warren family housed their slaves in the basement some time before 1827, when slavery was abolished in New York State. Over the years, the farmhouse was expanded, and it still exists. As late as the 1930s, the farm was part of a hunt trail.

Maple Cottage, January 1925
Lakeville Road in foreground
(New York Public Library)

John Dennelly, a later owner of the farm, was a descendant of Charles Carroll of Maryland, a signer of the Declaration of Independence. Dennelly was married to Catherine in 1876. Theirs was the first wedding at Great Neck's St. Aloysius Church, a wooden structure later to be replaced by the present-day building on Middle Neck Road in Great Neck's Old Village. Shortly thereafter, Dennelly bought the Warren farm, which had already been named Maple Cottage. His home was among the first in the area to have indoor plumbing and electric lights.

Field at Maple Cottage, January 1925
(New York Public Library)

Betty Wesstrom, Dennelly's granddaughter, visited her grandparents' home, in the 1930s, when she was a young child. Her fond recollections, in her own words, provide insight into the lifestyle of homeowners in Lake Success in the years before modern suburban development.

- *Acres of diverse property to roam*

- *Gigantic trees to hide Easter eggs under*

- *A forest of evergreens to play in*

- *The old barn with all the tack hanging so carefully in line*

- *The caretaker's cottage, Felix's, filled with china crocks … [containing] bones for the dogs and great pickles*

- *A big magnolia tree in the center circle of the front gravel drive*

- *Going to the brook to collect watercress for sandwiches*

- *Rooms filled with flowers all year, either from the gardens or the greenhouse*

- *Rooms filled with very beautiful antiques*

- *The living room had velvet covered finely carved Queen Anne [furniture]. Floral-striped wallpaper covered the walls.*

- *The dining room table sat twenty-four in beautiful carved Hepplewhite chairs. High sideboards were set with silver, one with silver pheasants, and a hunting scene dark-toned wallpaper covered the walls.*

- *A drop leaf table and chairs were set at one end of the dining room for daily tea. A three-tier serving piece held the sweets and little tea sandwiches.*

John and Catherine Dennelly and children, 1927
Golden wedding anniversary celebration
Note the picture of Theodore Roosevelt
(Courtesy, Betty Wesstrom)

After the Dennellys died, in the 1950s, their estate sold the farm and Maple Cottage. To the dismay of the heirs, the outer buildings were torn down and many homes were built on what the family considered small plots of land. One house could be seen from the next!

The eighteen-room home of Eddie Cantor, the entertainer, was built on ten acres in 1929, on what later became Pinehill Road. It was south of the Dennelly's. The young daughter of Cantor's chauffeur was a constant visitor at Maple Cottage. She always wished to live there and her wish came true when she grew up. She bought the house when it became available. Her family, the Kavanaughs, lived at Maple Cottage until some time in the 1970s.

Rear of Cantor house, 1929

Maple Cottage today looks very much the same as in days gone by. It has retained its old-fashioned charm amidst its modern-day surroundings.

Maple Cottage, 2000

William Kissam Vanderbilt II

William K. Vanderbilt II, more than any other Lake Success resident, has defined the character of the community. What were originally his private golf course and pool complex have evolved into the Village's public recreational facilities today.

W.K. Vanderbilt II
(Suffolk County Vanderbilt Museum)

Born in 1878, Willie K. was the great-grandson of Cornelius Vanderbilt, the railroad tycoon. Cornelius began his business venture in 1810 as the owner of one small boat used in a ferry service from Staten Island to Manhattan. This grew into an empire of ships and railroads.

In 1898, William was worth one hundred five million dollars, ten million more than in the national Treasury. For only one year, 1919, he was actively involved in the family business, as president of the New York Central Railroad. Vanderbilt's main interest was the sea. He sailed the world on his yacht, the Alva. He was a self-taught marine biologist. He collected samples of sea life, many of which were newly discovered species. These are on display at the Suffolk County Vanderbilt Museum. Vanderbilt donated the Alva to the Navy, at the beginning of World War II, for use in antisubmarine activity. In 1943, off the coast of New Jersey, a German submarine torpedoed the Alva.

At the turn of the twentieth century, wealthy New Yorkers, including Vanderbilt, were building summer homes on Long Island. He purchased the old Lakeville Hotel and a number of farms around the lake. He also bought Aunt Hannah's chicken shack. Because Vanderbilt was unable to obtain one parcel along the lake, the public still had access to the lake.

Vanderbilt built an interim house in 1902, with the intention of building a grander one on the shore of the lake, after he purchased the lake from the Town of North Hempstead. His goal was not achieved. The Town wanted $100,000 for the lake, but Vanderbilt was willing to pay only $50,000. When the sale did not occur, Vanderbilt remained in the original house, to which he added two very large wings.

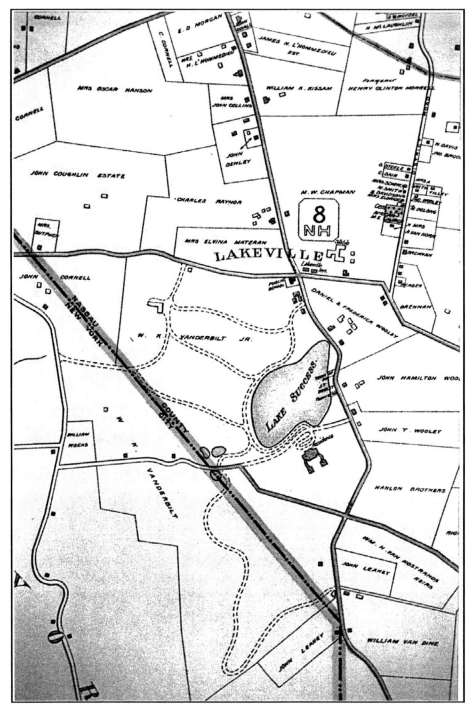

1906 map of Lakeville
Vanderbilt's property is shown, including internal roadways.
His residence is noted on the map, just below the lake.

Its thirty-eight rooms included twenty-two bedrooms, each with a private bath. French furniture, carpets, draperies and a large collection of paintings and etchings decorated the house. Outside, in the style of Versailles, a sunken garden contained a French fountain and statuary. An avenue of rhododendrons led to a Corinthian garden. There were greenhouses, fruit orchards, vineyards and vegetable gardens. Vanderbilt called this estate "Deepdale."

Vanderbilt home, 1904
(Suffolk County Vanderbilt Museum)

In 1908, the New York Times reported that Vanderbilt's "country seat," Deepdale, was leased to Paul Rainey, "polo player and yachstman." Parts of the estate were sold, beginning in 1913. Vanderbilt decided to build an estate in Centerport. He moved the Corinthian columns from his gardens in Lake Success to his new estate, where they can be seen today at the Suffolk County Vanderbilt Museum.

Vanderbilt home, 1905
(Suffolk County Vanderbilt Museum)

In 1925, the Glen Oaks Golf Club bought the mansion to serve as their clubhouse. After two years, they sold it because their members had too long a distance to walk, including having to cross over Marcus Avenue, to get from the golf course to their clubhouse. Subsequently, they built a clubhouse on their property in Queens. The mansion became a private home once again. Its two large wings were removed. Part of one wing was used to make a separate garage. Other alterations have been made. The house is on Westcliff Drive.

2003

In 1906, the south gate lodge of Deepdale was built in the Norman half-timber style. It stands today at 432 Lakeville Road, on the grounds of the St. Philip & St. James Church, alongside Long Island Jewish Medical Center.

*South gate lodge
2000*

In 1915, another lodge was built, to be used as a guest house. Eventually, it became the New York State police barracks along the Northern State Parkway, just west of Lakeville Road. It was torn down in 1967 when the parkway was widened.

*NY State Police Barracks,
circa 1935
(Nassau County Long Island
Studies Institute)*

South gate lodge and Church, 1953
Schumacher farm in foreground, now the site of LIJ
(North Shore Long Island Jewish Health System)

In 1923, Vanderbilt purchased an old cottage and farmland on Horace Harding Boulevard near the city line. In the early nineteenth century, the building temporarily housed slaves until they were transported to Manhattan. Vanderbilt made alterations and additions to the cottage. He built a swimming pool, an athletic field, and tennis and handball courts on the property.

William K. Vanderbilt II had been a Captain in the Navy in World War I, during which time he commanded a warship. Sometime in the 1920s, he made this property available to the 6th Battalion of the Naval Reserve for training and recreation. He placed a ship's gun in front of the farmhouse. It remains there to this day, in front of the police station.

In 1944, shortly after Vanderbilt's death, his estate sold the property to the Village. Located on its grounds are the Village pool, tennis courts, ball fields, and playground. The Village Hall was located in Vanderbilt's farmhouse until 1958, when it was relocated to the golf clubhouse. The police department and the courthouse remained in the old farmhouse until it was razed in the 1990s. They are now located in a new building that was erected on the same site. This building is also home to the Lake Success cooperative summer day camp.

Village Hall,
Police Station
and Court,
circa 1949

Village pool,
circa 1949
Replaced in 1956

Deepdale Golf Club

The rolling acres on the north side of the lake were ideal for a golf course. Golf was a favorite pastime of the wealthy men of William K. Vanderbilt's time. In 1926, on his estate, Vanderbilt built a two hundred acre golf course with a stucco clubhouse of Spanish design. Early players included Conde Nast and E. F. Hutton. Scenes for a W.C. Fields film, "So's Your Old Man," were filmed on the golf course during the summer of 1926.

The general design of the course was planned by Charles Macdonald, the father of golf course architecture. Seth Raynor, his protege, took charge of the on-site work. Some features of the course are attributed to Raynor. The seventeenth hole and several bunkers have retained their original design to this day.

Members of the Deepdale Club, 1926
William K. Vanderbilt II seated sixth from the left
(Suffolk County Vanderbilt Museum)

Vanderbilt sought permission from the Town of North Hempstead to use water pumped from Lake Success to irrigate the course. When his request was denied, he excavated to create a lake fed by Lake Success through a canal. He is reported to have said, "Surprise! I found a lake." Hence, the name Lake Surprise for the smaller lake just west of Lake Success.

Deepdale Golf Club, circa 1930
(Suffolk County Vanderbilt Museum)

In 1928, Vanderbilt sold the Deepdale Golf Club to a group of his friends for $1,600,000. The membership of the golf club increased over the years and the clubhouse was expanded. Many celebrities participated in the club's charitable events; among them were Dwight Eisenhower, Bob Hope, and Bing Crosby.

In 1931, nineteen-year old Lake Success resident Anthony Fieklecki, a recently licensed pilot, had a mishap while flying a biplane. He lost control and parachuted to safety, landing in a treetop on the Phipps estate. Sergeant Peterson, a Lake Success policeman, offered to bring a ladder, but Fieklecki climbed down unaided and uninjured. His plane fell into the waters of Lake Success. Golfers at the Deepdale Club were relieved that the plane didn't crash into their clubhouse. No one knows if the plane is still in the lake.

In 1952, New York State was making plans to build the Long Island Expressway. The path they proposed went right through the Village of Lake Success. Thirty-nine homes were to be demolished. The Lake Success Civic Association spearheaded the effort to change the route. At a meeting of residents, the Village engineer proposed an alternate plan that would straighten the expressway, making it 865 feet shorter. Only one house would be lost. Only one overpass would be necessary, instead of the three proposed. The cost would be reduced by two million dollars. Thirty-seven acres of Deepdale's golf course would be lost.

The State adopted the alternate plan. The Deepdale Club relocated to nearby North Hills. It sold what remained of its club in Lake Success to a realty firm in 1953. In 1955, plans to build homes on the former Deepdale Club site were announced. The Village Trustees proposed buying this property for Village use as a golf course. A one million dollar bond issue was approved by a vote of 349 to 232 and the land was purchased in 1956. At first, a nine-hole course was laid out. In 1958, by including previously unused land in the northwest section of the property, a complete 18-hole course was opened.

Shortly after the Village acquired the Deepdale Club, it utilized the clubhouse as the seat of Village government and also as a multipurpose facility for Village residents. In 1971, the clubhouse underwent a major renovation, with plans by Great Neck architect

Walter Blum, whose design won an award from the American Institute of Architects. Blum's sketch of the building appeared on Village stationery for thirty years.

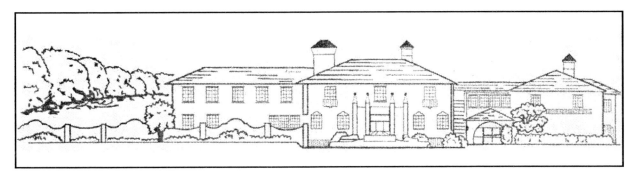

In the 1990s, the building no longer met the needs of the Village. The Trustees proposed a major reconstruction. After holding public meetings and a non-binding referendum, the Trustees approved the issuance of $8.3 million in bonds. The 1926 building was incorporated into the new structure, preserving elements of the original Spanish style.

Community building, 2003
Historic section in center

Vanderbilt's Long Island Motor Parkway

William K. Vanderbilt II had a fascination with the automobile. In 1889, when he was only eleven years old, he drove a car in Europe and in the United States. In January, 1904, he broke the world's speed record by going 92 miles per hour. Later in 1904, Vanderbilt organized a race on public roads in Nassau and Queens Counties. Thousands of spectators were present. The race became an annual event.

An account of the October 1905 automobile race was written by Agnes Dennelly of Maple Cottage, in Lake Success. Agnes wrote:

> The course included 23 miles, beginning at Mineola and passing through a number of towns on the south side of the island, thence toward Roslyn and Oyster Bay and thence toward Flaherty's corner [modern-day Lakeville Road and the Long Island Expressway] where we witnessed the race ... .

SOUVENIR , OF
NEW , YORK , AUTOMOBILE , SHOW
Madison Square Garden, January 13-20, 1906

The Royal on the Turn at Lakeville on the Long Island Course

1905 race at Flaherty's corner
Frank Flaherty, proprietor of the Lakeville Hotel
(Collection of Al Velocci)

Vanderbilt Cup Race, 1905
Lakeville Road, just south of today's Lake Road
Remnant of fence still present
(Collection of Howard Kroplick)

THE *Locomobile* MAKING AMERICA'S BEST RECORD IN ANY INTERNATIONAL COMPETITION.

The 90 H. P. Locomobile passing W. K. Vanderbilt, Jr.'s estate at Lakeville, L. I.

Vanderbilt Cup Race, 1905
Locomobile #7, on Lakeville Road, driven by Messrs. Tracy and Poole, guests at Maple Cottage
(Collection of Al Velocci)

When a spectator was killed at the third race, in 1906, Vanderbilt and his racing friends decided to build a private road for racing which would be available as a toll road for the general population. They formed the Long Island Motor Parkway Corporation for that purpose. Prominent among the directors were August Belmont, Harry Payne Whitney, John Jacob Astor, Henry Ford, and August Heckscher.

Construction of the Motor Parkway began in 1908, when one section was opened. By 1911, it ran from Flushing to Ronkonkoma, a distance of forty-eight miles. The roadway was built with a new material, Hassam paving, a form of reinforced concrete. It was only sixteen feet wide until 1926, when it was expanded to a width of twenty-two feet. This road became the nation's first limited access highway. It included sixty-five bridges, two underpasses and twelve toll lodges. There was no speed limit.

Typical view of Long Island Motor Parkway, circa 1910
(Nassau County Long Island Studies Institute)

From time to time, the road was closed to the general public while auto races were held. In 1910, after four spectators at a race were killed, newly adopted State legislation put an end to racing on the Long Island Motor Parkway. Thereafter, the road was used only as a toll road.

Vanderbilt was concerned about the overall appearance of the roadway. Trees and bushes were planted in a park-like setting. Vanderbilt sent John Russell Pope, a prominent architect, to France. Pope then designed each of the twelve toll houses in the style of French country homes, with stucco walls, steeply pitched roofs with dormers and large central chimneys. Shingled canopies were attached to the houses and sheltered the toll keepers as they leaned out the windows. At first, the toll was two dollars. Gradually, the toll was reduced until it was only forty cents in the 1930s. A yearly pass, affixed to one's car, like E-Z Pass, became available.

The Parkway, a road to nowhere, never made any money. Nassau and Suffolk Counties were sparsely settled. In the 1920s, as car use increased, the free Northern State Parkway was being planned. Vanderbilt offered to sell his roadway to New York State to be used for their parkway. Master planner Robert Moses refused the offer, saying that Vanderbilt's roadway was a dangerous "white elephant." In 1938, the Long Island Motor Parkway closed. Nassau and Suffolk Counties assumed ownership in lieu of taxes owed.

Looking west, in Lake Success: Northern State Parkway and Motor Parkway overpass, 1930s
(Collection of Howard Kroplick)

A half-mile section of Vanderbilt's parkway can be seen on the campus of the Great Neck South secondary schools. It has been covered with blacktop, except on the shoulders of the road, where original concrete remains. In a wooded area east of the football field, the road ends abruptly at the Northern State Parkway, where the abutment for a long-gone overpass is visible. Scattered about are the original black locust fence posts and connecting wire fencing which was used to keep livestock off the highway. To the west, this portion of roadway ends at Lakeville Road. In nearby Alley Pond Park and neighboring areas in Queens, more of the Motor Parkway and its overpasses can be seen.

Geese on Motor Parkway
near South High's football field

Two fence posts with attached wire,
from original Motor Parkway

When the roadway closed in 1938, Alex Greggo, who did maintenance work for Vanderbilt for forty years, purchased the toll house in Lake Success. His daughter, Ann, lived there until her death in the 1990s, when a new home was built on the site. It includes a now unrecognizable portion of the original toll house.

Of the original toll lodges, four remain, if only in part. One which has been restored to its original appearance now serves as headquarters for the Garden City Chamber of Commerce.

Buster, Scottie and the hens
Lake Success toll house, circa 1920
(Suffolk County Vanderbilt Museum)

Garden City toll lodge, 2001

Aerial view, 1952
North at the left

Long Island Motor Parkway overpass in left foreground, partially obscured by trees, continues at lower right
Overpass torn down in 1967, for the widening of Northern State Parkway to six lanes
Lakeville Road overpass, parallel to Motor Parkway, in center of photo
Both roads pass over the four-lane Northern State Parkway on the left
Marcus Avenue parallel to NSP on the right
Upper left: land cleared in readiness for development of Fawn Ridge (Tanners Road and Olive Street)

(UCLA Geography Air Photo Archives, 310-206-8188)

Henry C. Phipps

Born in Philadelphia in 1839, Henry C. Phipps was the son of a cobbler from England. Beginning as a bookkeeper, Phipps advanced in the business world until he was a partner with his childhood friend, Andrew Carnegie. Their venture later became the U.S. Steel Corporation.

Henry Phipps on left, with Andrew Carnegie

In 1901, Phipps sold his holdings in the Carnegie Steel Company to J. P. Morgan. Thereafter, he devoted his time to philanthropic causes. He established an organization, Phipps Houses, to build model tenements for the poor. The first buildings were on East 31st Street in what is now the Kips Bay area. Phipps Houses still exists today, owning and/or managing more than twelve thousand apartments for mixed-income families and for senior citizens. The New York Times, in its 1930 obituary of Phipps, reported that he donated more than seven million dollars to various charities. The actual amount is uncertain because many of his donations were given anonymously.

By 1914, Phipps, retired, was living on Fifth Avenue, overlooking Central Park. He fell ill and was confined to bed for most of the next fifteen years. His wife, Anne, decided they would leave Manhattan and move to the Gold Coast of Long Island. She purchased part of the Woolley farm. The land she acquired was just east of the lake.

Phipps administration building, Great Neck Public Schools, formerly Bonnie Blink
(Jessica Kovner Vega)

In 1916, she hired architect Horace Trumbauer to build a country house with white columns. The firm founded by Frederick Law Olmsted, who planned Central Park, was engaged to design the gardens. The name "Bonnie Blink" was given to the estate. Completed in 1917, the thirty-nine room Georgian mansion had two elevators, which were the first installed in a private home in the United States. One of these elevators is still being used today. On the grounds of the estate were stables, tennis courts, garages, and a barn amongst other buildings.

Henry Phipps died in 1930; his wife lived four more years. When their children, married, chose not to live in the family home, it remained empty until 1940. During the London blitz, thirty youngsters who were evacuated from England lived in the house under the supervision of Lady Margaret Barry of Norfolk, England. They remained at Bonnie Blink for three and one half years. The older children were sent to private schools while the younger ones were tutored at the house.

During World War II, an army unit was stationed at the eastern end of the Phipps estate. It was responsible for maintaining a flotilla of barrage balloons. The soldiers had an amicable relationship with the nearby farmers. They traded government-issue spices for local farm products.

After the war ended, the mansion was empty once again. In 1949, the Phipps heirs donated it and some of the grounds to the Great Neck School District. The stately exterior of the main house was kept intact. Its interior was converted for use as administrative offices. The marble floor and spiral staircase are reminders of its elegant past. In Phipps' wood-paneled study, once used for meetings of the Board of Education, hangs the original chandelier with one of its crystal birds. On Lakeville Road near South Middle School, one can see the original stone pillars marking the entrance to the estate.

Schools

At first, the education of children in Lake Success was the responsibility of School District #8, called Lakeville. The District encompassed a sparsely settled area south of what is now the railroad tracks. In 1932, District #8 disbanded and consolidated with District #7 to the north.

Daniel Stocker Woolley
1861-1949

In 1836, a one-room schoolhouse was built on land now the North Service Road of the Long Island Expressway, between Community Drive and Lakeville Road. Daniel S. Woolley, who later became a Trustee of the Village of Lake Success, attended this school. Woolley served on the school board of the Lakeville School District for forty years.

District #8 practiced segregation. A community of freed slaves and native Americans had been established in the 1820s in the vicinity of today's Community Drive. In 1867, the District built a one-room school, next to the A.M.E. Zion Church, for "colored children." The Church and the school district shared in construction expenses. The school, named "Institution U.S.A," was later known as the "colored school." The "white" and "colored" schools stood only a few hundred feet from each other. The "colored school" closed in 1909, when school segregation was no longer permitted in New York State.

The "white" school had forty-five students, taught by Miss Addie Hicks in the 1870s. In 1877, the "white" school was leveled as the result of a fire caused by children who were playing with firecrackers during their recess. An acre of land was bought from Charles and Louisa Van Nostrand to build a new eight-room, wood-frame school, located at what today is the southwest corner of Lakeville Road and the Long Island Expressway.

This was the Lakeville School. When the current Lakeville School was built, the first one became known as Old Lakeville. Additions to Old Lakeville were made over the years. It was used until 1929. It then stood empty until 1945, when the Village Engineer condemned the building as a fire hazard, and it was razed.

Old Lakeville School, undated
(Courtesy, Betty Wesstrom)

In 1928, the fourth school in Lake Success was built on five acres of land purchased from Howard Phipps. Named Lakeville School, it is in the northwestern part of Lake Success. A twelve-room building, with a gymnasium, auditorium, library, and cafeteria, opened in 1929. There were eighty children and four teachers for eight grades. Since then, the school has been enlarged. In 2003, its student population for grades one through five was seven hundred fifty, served by forty classroom teachers.

Lakeville School, 2003

In 1949, with the help of Myers E. Baker, a Great Neck realtor, School District #7 acquired, as a gift from the Phipps heirs, the Henry Phipps mansion along with nine acres of land. Soon after, the District acquired one hundred six more acres, part as an additional gift from the Phipps family, the remainder a donation from New York State.

A vote was held to approve the appropriation for the remodeling of the Phipps mansion into school district offices. The proposal passed by only three votes. In 1951, the District's administrative facilities moved from scattered quarters to the Phipps mansion. Many of the large rooms were partitioned to provide more office space. The butler's pantry, which contained a walk-in vault to safeguard the Phipps family silver, was used for the storage of school records.

Following World War II, a boom in residential construction led to an ambitious program to build new schools for the Great Neck School District. In 1951, one of the schools built was the permanent Parkville School in New Hyde Park. It served K-6 children in the southern part of Lake Success and in North New Hyde Park.

Parkville's original wooden building at the corner of Lakeville Road and Campbell Street was built in 1941 for use as army barracks to house military personnel working at the Sperry Gyroscope plant nearby. After the war, the builders Klein and Teichholz built the Lakeville Estates development of homes in North New Hyde Park. The barracks were converted into the area's elementary school. When the permanent building was erected in 1951, the wooden building, known as the "Annex," was still in service for the school children. After some years, the "Annex" was rented to the Great Neck Library for a branch facility still in use today.

The Cumberland School, in Lake Success, was also built in 1951, on eight acres of land formerly owned by Adelina Devendorf. It had twelve classrooms for grades K-3 and contained a concrete bomb shelter corridor for the "Cold War".

As time went by, the school district experienced declining enrollment. Several elementary schools were closed. The Cumberland School closed in 1976, Parkville in 1981. The Cumberland School now houses Great Neck's Adult Education program. Parkville School is now a kindergarten center for the Lakeville School population.

Ground was broken in 1955 for new junior and senior high schools on the former Phipps estate, with funds provided by a 7.9 million dollar bond issue. Labor disputes and a steel strike delayed completion of these schools until September 1958. Meanwhile, the existing secondary schools, soon to be the North schools, went on double sessions.

South Senior High School, above
South Middle School, left
2003

Lake Success is fortunate to have the 115-acre South school complex in its midst. Much of the original estate is preserved as natural woodlands, as stipulated by the Phipps heirs. Residents enjoy the running track, tennis courts and walking paths located on school grounds. They are also able to make use of an indoor pool at the Middle School. Most of all, they appreciate the fine education provided to their children.

Nathan S. Jonas

In the 1920s, Nathan Jonas, William Vanderbilt II and Henry Phipps were the biggest landowners in Lake Success. Jonas came from a humble background. At the age of thirteen, he left school to become an errand boy. He studied at night while working. He became a traveling salesman, selling baskets. Then he sold insurance. In 1905, Jonas founded the Citizens Trust Company which ultimately became the Manufacturers Trust Company through mergers. As its president, he introduced a profit-sharing program for the employees. It was an annual dividend of sixteen percent of salary.

Jonas at home in Lake Success, circa 1929

Jonas was very committed to civic and charitable activities. In 1909 he founded the Brooklyn Federation of Jewish Charities. He was the principal founder of Brooklyn Jewish Hospital. He was a member of the New York City Board of Education from 1902 to 1909. Jonas was active in the Democratic party, too, and was mentioned as a possible candidate for the mayor of New York City.

Jonas bought one hundred seventy acres of the Cox-Chapman farm from George Devendorf, in 1923, intending to build his estate there. Instead, he and a few of his friends built a golf course. The Lakeville Golf Club opened in 1925.

Shortly thereafter, Jonas bought an adjoining fifty-six acres, in the area now known as Wilshire. He built a mansion on what is now Grenfell Drive. He called it El Paraiso (paradise). It was built in the English country style. Twenty acres of informally land-scaped grounds surrounded the house. There were fountains and pools and a large rock garden. Full-grown rare trees were planted. Seedlings were cultivated in a nursery. Jonas, whose family came from Montgomery, Alabama, planted a boxwood garden in the southern style. A vegetable garden and fruit orchard provided enough for the family's needs. A greenhouse for orchids was especially dear to Mrs. Jonas.

Jonas mansion, circa 1929

Nathan Jonas suffered financially during the depression years. In 1931, he retired and sold his estate to George Devendorf. Jonas donated his prize orchids and other plants to the Brooklyn Botanic Garden. He moved to a smaller house in University Gardens. In 1940, he wrote his autobiography, "Through the Years," which is in the collection of the New York Public Library. Jonas died in 1943.

Adelina Devendorf offered to sell the former Jonas estate to the Great Neck School District in 1948. The offer was declined. The builders, Bowers and Effron, bought the property in 1949 and developed Wilshire, preserving many of the specimen trees which still stand. They demolished the Jonas mansion in 1950 but saved its roof tiles, which were used for two homes in Wilshire — one on Talbot Drive and the other on Grenfell Drive. The only surviving remnant of Jonas' magnificent gardens is a stone from his Japanese garden that can be seen on the front lawn of a house on Grenfell Drive.

Jonas as referee at historic bridge match, December 28, 1931
Left to right:
Sidney Lenz, Mrs. Eli Culbertson, Mr. Jonas, Oswald Jacoby, Eli Culbertson

Fresh Meadow Country Club

The Lakeville Golf Club, which Nathan Jonas and his friends established in 1925, flourished for a few years. Members included Eddie Cantor, the entertainer, Oscar Hammerstein, composer, Ring Lardner, writer, and James Farley, the U. S. Postmaster General. Franklin D. Roosevelt was an honorary member. During the depression, membership declined steadily. By 1940, the Prudence Bond Company foreclosed on the mortgage. The Lakeville Golf Club was out of business.

Lakeville Country Club, 1927
(Museum of the City of New York)

Just when the Lakeville Golf Club closed, the nearby Glen Oaks Golf Club was taken over by the U. S. Navy. Glen Oaks Golf Club extended from Little Neck Parkway to Lakeville Road, at the southern end of Lake Success. Today, the 33-story buildings of North Shore Towers occupy most of the site. In 1941, with the approach of World War II, the Navy built housing on the Glen Oaks site for military personnel brought in to join the thousands of civilians who were working at the Sperry Gyroscope plant. The displaced Glen Oaks golfers had the empty Lakeville course available to them. They leased it from the Prudence Bond Company and played golf there during the war years. In 1946, the Glen Oaks Club regained its course. The Lakeville property was empty once again, and Prudence sold it to the Fresh Meadow Golf Club of Queens.

Fresh Meadow Country Club has a history going back to 1896, when a group of wealthy German Jews formed the Unity Social Club in Brooklyn. In 1921, they purchased 106 acres of farmland in the Fresh Meadows area of Queens in order to build a golf course there. Nathan Jonas, a member, contributed generously and arranged loans and donations.

The Club flourished in Queens into the 1930s and 40s; however, its rural setting was disappearing as farms gave way to housing developments. Real estate values rose and taxes soared. New York City had plans to lay a sewer line across the fairway. It was time to move. Many of their members had moved to Long Island from Brooklyn and Manhattan, so they looked for a location to the east. The golf course in Queens was sold and developed into housing, a movie theater and a shopping center in the vicinity of 188th Street. The defunct Lakeville Club became their new home, and the name of the club in Lake Success became Fresh Meadow Country Club.

Fresh Meadow Country Club, 2003

Incorporation of the Village of Lake Success

The area now called Lake Success was known as Lakeville since the early nineteenth century. By the 1920s, large estates, golf courses and farms were present. The largest estates belonged to Vanderbilt, Phipps and Jonas. The golf clubs were Deepdale, Glen Oaks and Lakeville.

The lake, particularly in summer, attracted large numbers of people who came to swim and fish. The North Hempstead Record of August 4, 1926, reported:

> This summer, conditions at the lake have been worse than ever before, and complaints by the score have been registered with Town Clerk Mullon of alleged indecencies committed, of noisy bathing parties and scantily clad youths disporting themselves on the highway to the annoyance of motorists. It is rapidly becoming a miniature Coney Island, and instead of a spot of beauty is assuming the proportions of an eye-sore.

Nathan Jonas was a leader in the drive for incorporation of the area so that zoning regulations could be enacted to keep outsiders away from the lake. Two contiguous incorporated villages were proposed. The dividing line between them was approximately where the Long Island Expressway is today.

To the north, on December 8, 1926, voting was held on the issue of incorporation of the Village of Lakeville. The voting took place at the Lakeville Golf Club. The population of this area was eighty-four. Incorporation was defeated by a vote of eleven to nine.

To the south, where the population was sixty-eight, on December 14, 1926, incorporation of the Village of Success was approved in a vote held at the Deepdale Golf Club. The Village of Success, half the size of present-day Lake Success, had only eleven taxpayers — all of them wealthy.

Thorne House, built in 1826, served as the first Village Hall. It was the home of the greens keeper for the Deepdale Golf Club and later for the Lake Success Golf Club. In 1964, it was torn down and a new home was constructed in its place.

Thorne House, January 1925 (New York Public Library)

By a vote of four to zero, the unincorporated area of Lakeville was added to the Village of Success on December 30, 1927. A proposition to change the name from Success to Lake Success was also approved. The first Mayor was Edmond Frisch and the two Trustees were Blanche Frisch and Daniel S. Woolley.

Incorporation gave the Village of Lake Success the power to establish local zoning ordinances. Early ordinances prohibited cattle, horses, swine and goats from running at large. There was also a ban on fat rendering. In January 1928, the Village passed an ordinance to ban nude bathing and parking around the lake. This kept outsiders away from the lake and restored peace and quiet to the community.

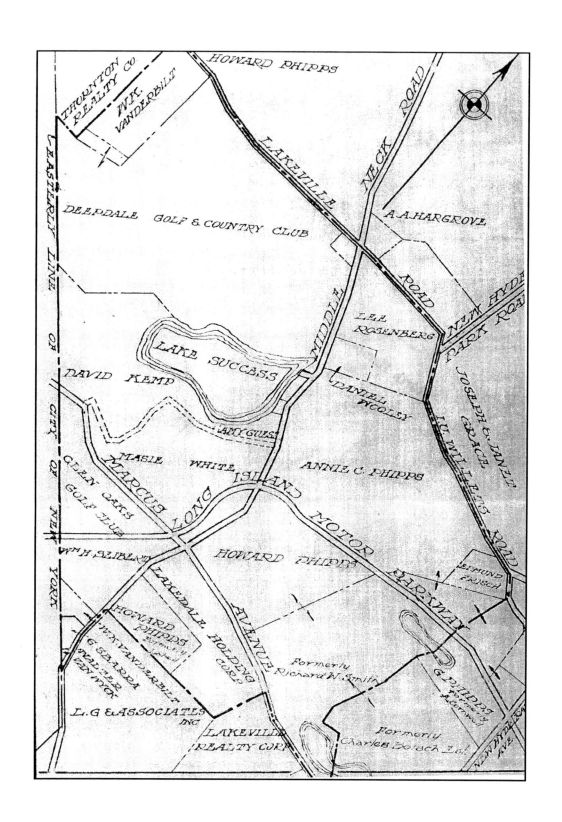

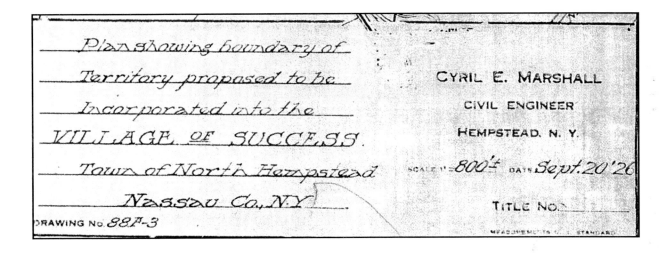

Map used for incorporation of the Village of Success, September 1926
Lakeville Road, then, ran east to west (now, Horace Harding Boulevard/ North Service Road)
Middle Neck Road, then, is Lakeville Road today
Lakeville Road, then, was northern boundary of the proposed Village of Success

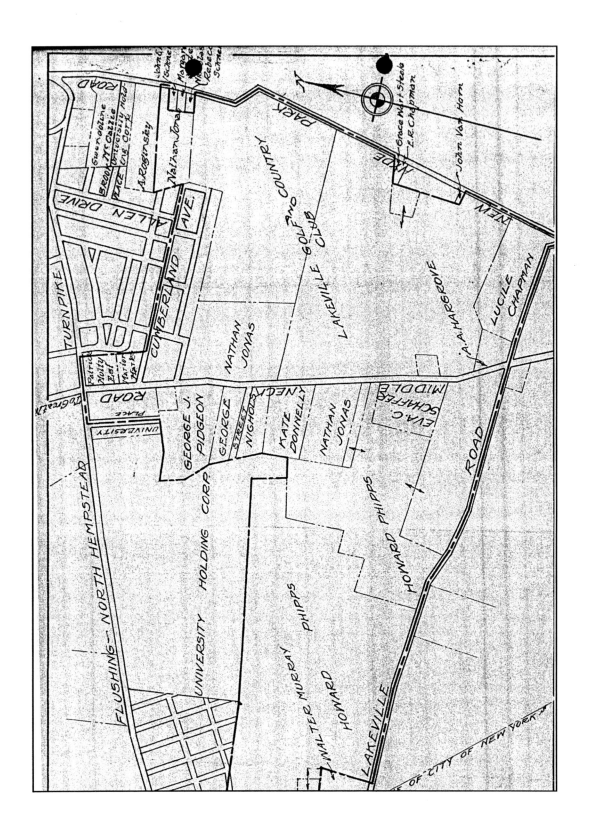

60

Plan showing boundary of
territory proposed to be
annexed to the _____
VILLAGE OF SUCCESS
Town of North Hempstead,
Nassau Co., N.Y. _____
WING No. 88F-2

CYRIL E. MARSHALL

CIVIL ENGINEER

HEMPSTEAD. N. Y.

SCALE 1" = 800'± DATE Feb. 15, 1927

TITLE No. _____

MEASUREMENTS U. S. STANDARD

NS BLUE PRINT WORKS

Map used to include unincorporated Lakeville into the Village of Success,
February 1927
Nathan Jonas property to the west of Middle Neck Road was later owned by Eddie Cantor
"Kate Donnelly" was Catherine Dennelly of Maple Cottage

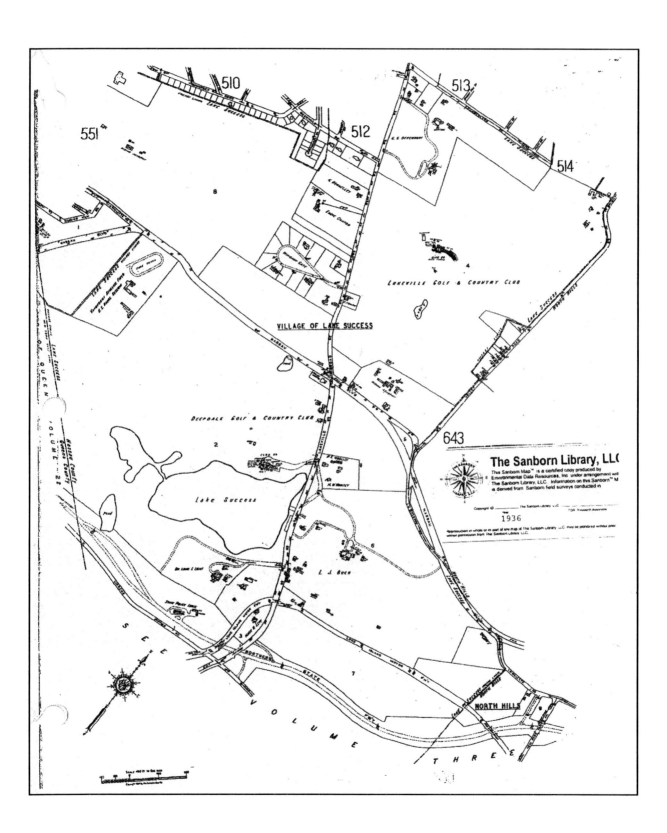

1936 map

Compare to the 1926 and 1927 maps:

The "old" Lakeville Road is now called Nassau Boulevard
The "old" Middle Neck Road is now called Lakeville Road

State Police Lodge (formerly Vanderbilt lodge) adjoins Northern State Parkway

Vanderbilt property on today's Horace Harding Boulevard is noted on map

Windsor Gate has come into being

Riding Academy in northwest corner is Rice farm

Old Lakeville School (labeled "Police") at southwest corner of Lakeville Road and Nassau Boulevard

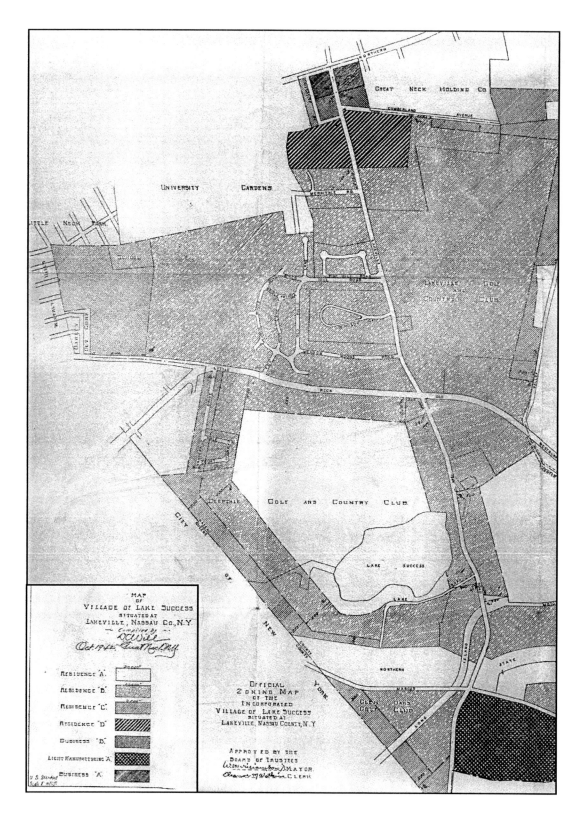

MAP
OF
VILLAGE OF LAKE SUCCESS
SITUATED AT
LAKEVILLE, NASSAU CO., N.Y.
Compiled by
D.C. Will
Oct. 1942. Great Neck N.Y.

RESIDENCE "A."
RESIDENCE "B."
RESIDENCE "C."
RESIDENCE "D."
BUSINESS "B."
LIGHT MANUFACTURING "A."
BUSINESS "A."

OFFICIAL
ZONING MAP
OF THE
INCORPORATED
VILLAGE OF LAKE SUCCESS
SITUATED AT
LAKEVILLE, NASSAU COUNTY, N.Y.

APPROVED BY THE
BOARD OF TRUSTEES
, MAYOR.
, CLERK.

64

Official zoning map, October 1942

Compare to the 1936 map:

There are new streets in the Meadow Woods Road area

Also new, Birch Hill/Pine Hill Road, Merrivale Road,
Vanderbilt Drive/Dale Carnegie Court, and Lake Road

Nassau Boulevard now called Little Neck Old Westbury Road

Sperry Gyroscope Corporation property is at the bottom (dark area)

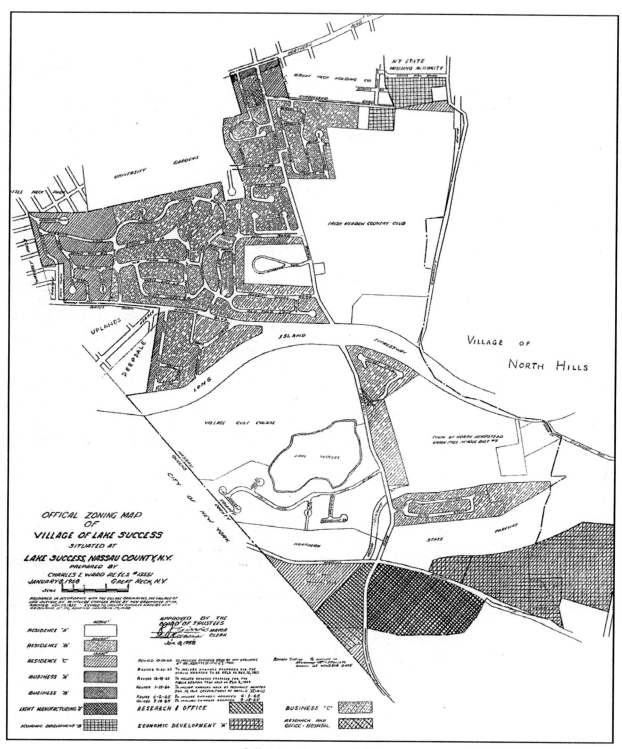

Official zoning map, 1958

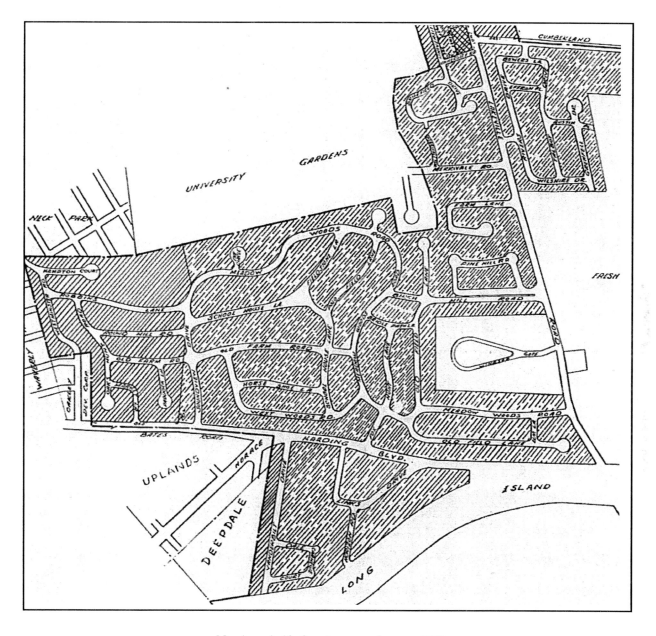

Northern half of zoning map, January 1958

Compare to the 1942 map:
All present-day streets in existence
Long Island Expressway built

Street names in the vicinity of the Rice horse farm:
Paddock, Horseshoe, Bridle Path, Polo Field,
reminders of Village history.

Police

Upon incorporation in 1927, the Village of Lake Success hired its first constable, James Peterson; he patrolled on foot. Peterson was also employed as a chauffeur for a local attorney. His duties as a police officer were to keep cars from parking along the roads and to keep nonresidents off the lake. He worked an eight-hour day, albeit any eight hours he chose. The police headquarters was in a barn on Vanderbilt farm land.

In 1929, a second policeman was hired. A motorcycle with sidecar and a second-hand automobile were purchased for use by the police force. In 1932, there were four police officers and all-night protection was provided. In 1930, a police building, only six feet by six feet, was erected at what is now the corner of Lakeville Road and the Long Island Expressway. It was demolished in the 1950s when the Long Island Expressway was built. Before it was torn down in 1945, the old Lakeville School was also used by the police department.

Police booth, 1930s

After William Vanderbilt II died in 1944, the Village purchased his property on Horace Harding Boulevard. The farmhouse on the land became the police station. The Village Hall was upstairs until 1958. The police station is at the same site today, but in a new building constructed in 1998.

Original Vanderbilt cottage and dining porch before alterations, circa 1944

Police/Courthouse, 1960s
Vanderbilt ship's gun visible in both photos

During World War II, a civilian volunteer fire corps was established. At war's end, the corps was transformed into a volunteer police emergency squad of twenty men. Through donations from members of the squad and other residents, a fully equipped truck and rowboat were purchased. The squad was trained to respond to natural disasters, traffic accidents and household emergencies. The emergency squad was disbanded in 1985.

Police Emergency Squad, circa 1960

The police department has grown to keep pace with the increasing population. The Village now employs twenty-three police officers. They use six patrol cars which log over 120,000 miles a year. Lake Success is one of only twelves villages in Nassau County which have their own 911 emergency service. Approximately one-third of the Village budget is for police protection. Residents of Lake Success enjoy the comfort and security of having their own responsive police force.

Sperry Gyroscope Corporation

Many well-known Lake Success families have owned the 120-acre property bounded by Lakeville Road, Union Turnpike, New Hyde Park Road and Marcus Avenue. Among them are Cornell, Hicks, Seaman, Van Nostrand, Williams, Woolley and Kissam. Part of the site is in the Village of Lake Success; the rest is in an unincorporated area in the Town of North Hempstead.

Elmer Sperry
1860-1930

Shortly before the United States entered into World War II, the Defense Plant Corporation, a federal agency, bought the property from Fred Schumacher, Jr., and the Tanners Pond Corporation, with the intention of constructing a plant to manufacture war materials. The Sperry Gyroscope Corporation planned to lease and operate the plant for the government.

On May 2, 1941, Sperry applied to the Village of Lake Success for a zoning variance which would permit the erection of a factory, "a modern structure to employ 7,000 people." Objections were raised. A legal action to prevent issuance of a building permit failed. War needs overrode other considerations.

To lessen the impact on residents, there were height restrictions and buffer areas using trees and shrubs. Ground was broken on July 8, 1941; a sprawling complex with over two million square feet of floor space was built. The manufacture of precision instruments and controls began in 1942. In particular, bomb sights and gun turrets for B-17 and B-24 bombers were produced.

In order to provide protection against air attack, in 1943, a Barrage Balloon Battalion of the Army Coast Artillery was stationed in the woods on the Phipps estate just to the north of the factory. Barrage balloons were also placed in Glen Oaks and New Hyde Park. Fortunately, no enemy airplanes tested this defense system, since it was later shown to be ineffective.

During World War II, the nearby Glen Oaks Golf Course was taken over by the military. Temporary housing was constructed there for military personnel who worked at the plant. At the height of activity, about 20,000 people were employed.

Artist's rendering of factory floor during World War II
(Nassau County Long Island Studies Institute)

Helen Sperry Lea, Lake Success resident and daughter of the founder of Sperry Gyroscope, together with other property owners, recognized the need for housing for Sperry employees. They sought a zoning variance to downgrade thirty-six acres so garden apartments could be constructed in the Lake Road area. The Lake Success Civic Association was successful in its opposition to the plan.

At war's end, production at the plant was scaled back. In 1951, the Federal government sold the property to the Sperry Gyroscope Corporation for eleven dollars. Henceforth, work was done for the government and for private enterprise, in such fields as aviation and radio.

In 1986, when Sperry merged with Burroughs to form Unisys Corporation, 4,500 workers were employed at the Marcus Avenue facility. In 1996, Lockheed Martin Corporation became the owner. Its primary focus was the development of navigation systems for the Navy's Trident nuclear submarine, using the ponds on the property to test submarine devices. In December, 1998, Lockheed Martin shut down its operation in Lake Success

Lockheed Martin sold its property in 2000 to i.park, which transformed the former defense plant into a hi-tech business center for various tenants. i.park modernized the original Sperry buildings. It landscaped the property and built a soccer field for public use. In its lobby, on Marcus Avenue, is an exhibit of photos and documents which recall the historic significance of the site as a defense plant and as a temporary home of the United Nations.

The United Nations in Lake Success

By 1945, the temporary quarters of the United Nations at Hunter College in the Bronx had become inadequate, and other sites were sought. The Sperry Gyroscope Corporation offered part of its facility in Lake Success as a temporary home for the U. N.

Many residents objected to the loss of $323,000 in tax revenue. They worried also about an increase in traffic. They wanted to maintain a quiet suburban life. Mayor Van Bloem arranged for the U. N. to make an annual payment in lieu of local taxes. A non-binding referendum was held. Voters were asked, *"Shall the citizens of Lake Success welcome and cooperate with the U. N. in its temporary occupancy of the Sperry plant?"* The favorable result was 102 to 70. The United Nations moved to Lake Success on August 16, 1946.

James O'Neill, Lake Success resident, receiving check for one dollar from U.N. officials as payment to his moving company for moving the U.N. from Hunter College to Lake Success February 28, 1947 (United Nations Photo Library)

All branches of the United Nations except the General Assembly were housed in Lake Success. The General Assembly met at an ice skating rink which had been part of the 1939 World's Fair in Flushing Meadows, Queens. World leaders who came to Lake Success included Eleanor Roosevelt (U.S.), George Marshall (U.S.), Andrei Gromyko (Russia), Lester Pearson (Canada), Carlos Romulo (Phillipines), and Clement Attlee (Great Britain).

Security Council in Lake Success, June 30, 1947
(United Nations Photo Library)

Eleanor Roosevelt in Lake Success, November 1949
(United Nations Photo Library)

Many important issues arose while the United Nations met in Lake Success. When mainland China was taken over by the Communists, a controversy arose: Would Taiwan retain its seat as the representative of China? When the Security Council decided in favor of Taiwan, Andrei Gromyko, in protest, staged the first walkout in U.N. history.

In 1947, the Palestine Committee was formed. In the spring of 1948, it concluded its study, recommending to the General Assembly that Palestine be partitioned into separate Jewish and Arab states. The General Assembly agreed to this partition by more than a two-thirds vote. On May 14, 1948, in Lake Success, the Security Council approved a proclamation recognizing the independence of Israel.

In June, 1950, North Korea invaded South Korea. On June 27, the Security Council approved the use of military force, primarily American, to defend South Korea. This action was never officially called a war: It was a "police action."

United Nations in Lake Success, circa 1948
Fifty-one flags of member nations

Schumacher house, on Sperry property, built as a one-room house approximately 300 years ago
Used as a guest house by Sperry Gyroscope, 1941-46
Housed U.N. nursery school
Building later moved to its current location at Clinton Martin Park, New Hyde Park

Employees of the United Nations found it difficult to secure housing. None lived in Lake Success, where there were no multi-family dwellings. Non-white personnel experienced racial discrimination. The United Nations arranged the construction of several housing developments, one of which was Parkway Village, on Main Street in Queens.

A four-man police force had been adequate for 800 Lake Success residents. The presence of the United Nations resulted in an increase to eight police officers. There were some problems with demonstrations in the U.N. parking lots, with rush hour traffic, and also with speeding limousines whose drivers claimed diplomatic immunity. In 1948, a small plane flew over U.N. headquarters and detonated a stick of dynamite attached to a long wire. The pilot, who was later arrested, declared that he was trying to awaken the delegates to their responsibilities in a troubled world.

One day a year was declared U.N. Day in the Village. On that day, the United Nations tennis team played against Lake Success residents on the Village's two tennis courts. It has been reported that Trygve Lie, the Secretary General, presented the winner's cup. The tennis matches continued into the 1960s.

A total of 8,266 meetings were held in Lake Success in five years. There were more than 1,600,000 visitors and 3,000 employees. The names **United Nations** and **Lake Success** were linked in world history.

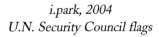

i.park, 2004
U.N. Security Council flags

A plaque was placed at the former entrance to the United Nations on Marcus Avenue. It can be seen today in the lobby of the i.park complex.

1945–1951 HEADQUARTERS OF
THE UNITED NATIONS
AND ITS WORLD WIDE ACTIVITIES FOR PEACE
MARKER ERECTED BY
TOWN OF NORTH HEMPSTEAD
UNITED NATIONS DAY, OCTOBER 24, 1965

These players participated in the tennis match between Lake Success and the United Nations at the Lake Success Village Green Saturday, Aug. 26. From left, kneeling: Paul Solomon (LS), Steve Gallin (LS), Sig Warshow (LS), Dave Chandler (LS), Joe Struhl (LS), Murray Rose (LS), Ali Shams (UN), M. Chien (UN), John Jahoda (UN), J. Lorenz (UN), C. Coleridge (UN), J. Crouzet-Pascal (UN). Standing, same order, Milt Dillon (LS), Alan Berk (LS), Marv Sinkoff (LS), Eric Adler (LS), Victor Baum (LS), Jeff Schutzer (LS), Sy Luba (LS), Dick Lewis (LS), Mickey Neuwirth (UN), Virgil DiAngelis Solomon (Captain, LS), Harry Abrahams (LS), Allee Sinkoff (LS), Dan Klausner (LS), Harriet Struhl (LS), Elizabeth Bloomfield (UN), T. Nyien (UN), Winifred Chien (UN), J. Chapman (UN), Tom DeCandia (UN), A. Bovay (UN), C. Woods (UN), R. Mairata (UN), H. Oppenheimer (UN), Luis Marques (Captain, UN), S. Zotos (UN).

In a thrilling three-hour mixed match, Berk and Lewis defeated Marques and Crouzet-Pascal of the UN team 3-6, 6-2 and 12-10; Solomon and Struhl defeated Nylen and Shams of the UN team 6-2, 7-5; Baum and Klausner defeated Coleridge and Woods in another long match 13-15, 6-3, 6-3; and in a mixed doubles A. Sinkoff and E. Adler defeated J. Chefetz and R. Mairata 6-4, 1-4, 7-5. The event ended in a 4-4 tie, with the ninth match unable to be played because of rain.

Miyata Photo

Lake Success and United Nations tennis teams, 1961
(Photo and caption, courtesy of the Great Neck Record)

Development along Marcus Avenue

Joseph Ridder purchased fifty-five acres of land from the Phipps estate in 1959. The property was called Tanners Pond. It extended from Marcus Avenue to the Northern State Parkway, between Lakeville Road and New Hyde Park Road.

By 1962, many homes had been built in nearby Manhasset Hills. When Ridder proposed industrial development for his property, homeowners in Manhasset Hills and some in Lake Success united in their opposition under the name Manhasset Hills Council.

The Village of Lake Success hired four planning consultants in 1962. They recommended industrial zoning. Their rationale was that Ridder's property was adjacent to a commercial area and in a location with heavy traffic. They believed these factors were not conducive to residential housing consistent with development in Lake Success.

Some Lake Success residents favored industrial development so the residential tax burden would be lessened. They joined together as "The Lake Success Committee for Lower Taxes and Higher Property Values." They pointed out that Village taxes had increased 600% in the previous twenty years. Furthermore, the feelings were that if the property had already been commercially developed, it would have generated 25% of the 1963-64 tax revenue.

On September 16, 1963, the Lake Success Board of Trustees acted on the recommendation of its Planning Board and adopted a resolution which rezoned Tanners Pond from Residence C to Economic Development Zoning A. This permitted light manufacturing plants and office buildings.

The Nassau County Planning Commission held a hearing. Many Village residents appeared to support commercial development. The Manhasset Hills Council was strongly opposed. The Nassau County Planning Commission approved industrial zoning on February 18, 1964.

The Ridder estate sold the property to We're Associates, who erected six buildings. Regulations about plot size, building height, maximum land coverage, and landscaping assured an attractive appearance.

3000 Marcus Avenue

In 1971, the Village rezoned another parcel of land, also along Marcus Avenue but west of Lakeville Road. Twenty acres of the former Glen Oaks Club, which had moved to Old Westbury in the early 1970s, were now zoned for business use. There was no community opposition. Office building were erected.

Sigmund Sommer owned 106 acres, which was the remainder of the golf course. He built North Shore Towers, three 32-story luxury apartment buildings, on a portion of the land which was in New York City. The land in Lake Success was used for a reconfigured golf course for residents of the Towers.

The Harbor Hill Sanctuary

Hidden in the Village of Lake Success, just south of Lake Road, along Lakeville Road, is a 4.4 acre nature preserve. In 1967, when Helen Sperry Lea moved to Bellport, she donated her land in Lake Success to the Nature Conservancy. Lea was the daughter of the founder of the Sperry Gyroscope Company. From 1909 to 1914, she helped her father and brother to develop gyroscope technology to hold airplanes steady in flight. She and her brother went on unsteady test flights until the equipment was perfected. Helen and her husband, an engineer for the Sperry Company, bought a home which was originally used as servants' quarters for Deepdale, the estate of William K. Vanderbilt II. Extensive alterations transformed its appearance. Lea had hoped to donate her home to the Nature Conservancy. They declined the offer because of the expense of upkeep of the house. The house is privately owned, at the end of a long driveway from Lake Road.

The nature preserve, called Harbor Hill Sanctuary, lies on the Harbor Hill Terminal Moraine of the Wisconsin ice sheet. The sanctuary contains a station to monitor bird populations. Its workstation is a converted chicken coop from Vanderbilt's Deepdale estate, which was famous for its poultry. In the spring and fall, food and water are set out to attract migrating birds. The birds are caught without harm in nets. The species, sex and age of each bird is noted and a band is placed on the bird's leg before it is released.

This sanctuary is part of a nationwide network of 2500 sites that contribute to a database at the Bird Banding Laboratory of the U.S. Geological Survey in Laurel, Maryland. When a change in bird population is observed, an investigation is conducted to determine the cause. The harmful effects of DDT were brought to light in such a study.

Helen Sperry Lea's belief in open space preservation has continued in her family. In 2003, her son, Sperry Lea, sold his property in Bellport for public use. The property includes a skating pond and wetlands near Great South Bay.

Lake Success Today

Lake Success has long been populated because of its natural resources. Native Americans hunted in its forests and fished its lakes. The Dutch and English farmed here. Wealthy homeowners built estates and golf courses as this area became part of the Gold Coast of Long Island. In time, the estates were broken up and homes were built on smaller parcels. By the 1950s, almost all available land had been used.

The Village of Lake Success is a desirable residential area convenient to Manhattan. Approximately three thousand residents live in the 1.8 square mile community. In 1940, the population was only 203. Most homes are on lots that are at least one-quarter acre.

Many residents believe the Village is defined by its recreational facilities. These include an 18-hole golf course, two swimming pools, eleven tennis courts, two ball fields, a basketball court, and a playground for young children. A summer nursery camp, run by parents, has been in existence since 1954. As many as seventy-five children, aged three to six, are in their own wing in the new Police/Court/Recreation building.

Police/Courthouse and Village pool, 2002

Labor Day weekend at the Village Green, 2003
Children's activities included pony rides, petting zoo
and carnival in the playground

The new community building at the golf course is a focal point of Village life. Its elegantly furnished lobby is paneled with the wooden doors of the original lockers of the Deepdale Club. In it is a restaurant, the Grill Room, for residents and their guests. Its very large multi-purpose room overlooks the lake. Meetings of Village government and Village organizations are held here. Residents play cards here. This room, which can accomodate approximately three hundred people, is available for catered parties. Also in the building is a fitness center for the residents, a sauna, and locker rooms for use by golfers and members of the fitness center. The building also houses the municipal offices.

Lobby and Grill Room

The Village of Lake Success is governed by a Mayor and six Trustees, elected for two-year terms. At the present time, there is only one political party, the Village Party, which holds a convention every spring to nominate candidates for office. Advising the Board of Trustees are three commissions: Environment, Golf and Park. A Planning Board and a Board of Zoning Appeals deal with applications for renovations and new construction. An elected Justice presides for infractions of local laws. A Village Administrator/Clerk oversees all aspects of Village operations. The Village has its own police force and its own Department of Public Works. It provides garbage pickup six days a week.

The Lake Success Civic Association has been in existence since 1942, when the community needed a voice to oppose the development of multi-family dwellings. Today, the Civic Association describes it purpose in its bylaws: "to take active and continued inter-est in Village problems in a non-partisan manner; to culti-vate social intercourse among its members." It hosts a holi-day party in December and organizes other programs dur-ing the year. Its Garden Committee plants and maintains traffic islands in the Village.

Lake Success residents of all ages enjoy the services of the Village and benefit as well from fine schools, libraries, shops and a Senior Center in Great Neck. Many young families have purchased homes in the Village. Houses are undergoing major renovations or are being torn down and replaced by large homes with very different architectural styles than those of fifty years ago. The look of the Village is changing. We can admire the new but we must remember, respect, and preserve our past.

End Notes

Photographs are treasures of history. Present-day photos without credits were taken by the author, who has enjoyed his status as amateur photographer for many years. Another amateur photographer whose work appears is Eugene L. Armbruster, a manufacturer of cigar boxes. After he retired in 1920, Armbruster traveled the length and breadth of Long Island, photographing rural scenes. He hiked as many as eighteen miles a day on farm roads. In this book, his photos all bear the credit of New York Public Library. They are held in the Milstein Division of United States History, Local History & Genealogy, Astor, Lenox and Tilden Foundations.

Photographs credited to Suffolk County Historical Society were taken by Hal B. Fullerton. Fullerton was so excited by the natural beauty of Long Island that he called it the "blessed isle." His love of Long Island and his professional skills met the needs of the Long Island Railroad, which employed him from 1897 to 1927. His photos appeared in newspapers in order to encourage LIRR ridership. In the late 1940s, 2500 glass plates and lantern slides of Fullerton's work were rescued from a trash barrel and donated to Suffolk County Historical Society.

The pen and ink sketches were drawn by Robert Danzer. Danzer purchased one of the first Newell and Daniel homes in Lake Success in 1940. He became the Village Historian and wrote a history of Lake Success, published in 1949. With his wife, Helen, he painted a large "illuminated history" of Lake Success, which hangs in the office of the Mayor today. In 2002, Danzer met with the author to reminisce about Lake Success in the 1940s. Danzer recalled buying onions at a farm stand on Lakeville Road, attending horse shows at the Rice farm, and going to the swimming beach at the lake.

The author appreciates the help he received from friends and neighbors. In particular, he thanks Greg Leong, Carol Bernstein, Lea Glickman, Mayor Robert Bernstein, Fred Handsman, Betty Wesstrom, Howard Kroplick, Al Velocci, Leila Matteson and Risha Rosner from the Reference Department of the Great Neck Library, Florence Ogg of the Suffolk County Vanderbilt Museum, and Wallace Broege of the Suffolk County Historical Society.

Lakeville House
"Drawn from Nature by G. Hayward," 1839

Lake Road, circa 1902
(Suffolk County Vanderbilt Museum)

Incorporated Village of Lake Success
318 Lakeville Road
Lake Success, New York 11020

Robert Bernstein, Mayor
Stephen Lam, Deputy Mayor

Trustees:
Ronald Cooper
Fred Handsman
Adam Hoffman
Robert Kraus
Richard Sondak

Dr. Jack Binder
Village Historian